# THE SCREW CITY POEMS
### (and a few odds and ends)

## by Richard Vargas

# ROADSIDE PRESS

Cover Photography: Mark Bond
Editor: Michele McDannold

Roadside Press
Colchester, IL

Acknowledgments: All poems and the essay excerpt have been published in the titles listed below. The only pieces that are previously unpublished is the poem, *not in the job description*, and the fictional work-in-progress. I thank the editors of all poetry journals and lit mags who accepted and published my work over the years. Your efforts to keep the small press alive and well wherever you are will always be appreciated.

Part I: *McLife*, Main Street Rag Press, 2005 (out of print)
*(not in the job description*, The Chiron Review, Winter 2025)

Part II: *American Jesus*, Tia Chucha Press, 2007 (out of print)

Part III: *Guernica, revisited*, Press 53, 2014

Part IV: *How A Civilization Begins*, Mouthfeel Press, 2022

Part V: *leaving a tip at the Blue Moon Motel*, Casa Urraca Press, 2023

# Table of Contents

# Introduction

I am at an age when some poets get lazy and decide it's time for the "New and Selected" collection of their work. Those of us who are smiled upon by the big publishing houses (don't look at me) most likely get gentle nudges to just do it and generate some quick book sales. It's doesn't take a lot of sweat and tears to put together about twenty-percent unpublished poems that are then padded with poems previously published in their books from years gone by. What they consider to be their "hits," along with a few misses. In my case, it's merely an opportunity to present a sampling of my writing from the beginning to the present for those who have not read all my books. Has anyone read all of them? Buy that reader a beer.

As I began to sort through my five books of poetry, getting a feel for the poems I thought had the potential to be included in my "New and Selected," it became apparent that much of my earlier work had one shared trait; they all had a connection to the people and places associated with Rockford, Illinois.

My earliest memory of hearing about Rockford was during the mid-1970s as a student wandering around the halls at Cal State University, Long Beach, trying to make up my mind if I wanted to pursue a degree in criminal justice, or English with an emphasis on creative writing. I still lived at home while commuting to campus, and one day my brother walked into my room holding up a new album he had just purchased by a hot new band getting major airtime on all the FM rock stations with their song titled, *California Man*. "And get this," he said, "they are from someplace called 'Rockford.'"

Jump ahead to 1979, the year after I graduated from CSULB. My one (and only) DUI led to a decision to get away from smoking too much pot and cracking open my first beer of the day by 10 a.m. Joining the Army provided the radical change of course I deemed necessary at that time, and it probably saved my life. I had completed almost 18 months of training and attending various schools (to include Officer Candidate School and jump school) at Ft. Benning, GA, and was finally assigned to Ft. Carson, CO to begin my duties as a rookie infantry lieutenant. I met the woman who I would ask to marry me, and we tied the knot in 1981. And she was raised in Rockford.

My initial introduction to Rockford were the annual week-long visits with my in-laws. We spent most of the time on the westside. My impression was that the town was depressed, economically and culturally. If someone had told me that one day I would live there, I would have said, "no fucking way." I left the army in 1983 and we moved to So. California to stake our claim.

But shit happens. Due to the implosion of my family that was having a damaging effect on our marriage, my ex and I made the decision to leave So. California and relocate to be closer to my in-laws. After residing for twelve years in Orange County where we were a short drive from Disneyland and Huntington Beach, we left the Golden-but-tarnished state in May 1995, and moved to the home of Cheap Trick. Culture shock did ensue. Upon asking to be seated in the no smoking section of a local eatery, I was left shaking my head when I was directed to the two tables at the back of the room where I was surrounded by smokers. And don't even get me started on the drivers!

I should mention that prior to making the move, I had been struggling to kickstart my writing for 15 years. Upon joining the military, I assumed my time in the army would provide plenty of writing material and my poetry would thrive. The opposite happened, and the beginning of a severe writer's block frustrated me for over a decade.
Within a few months after settling in our new home, I found myself sitting in with a group of writers meeting at the Ethnic Heritage Museum on So. Main St. No one knew me. I could reinvent myself. I could be anyone or anything I wanted to be. I could have said I was a former hit man for the CIA or someone in the witness protection program. Who was going to challenge me? Instead, I returned to my true self;

I started to write poetry. And the words began to flow from my fingertips. I made new friends and started hanging around with (as my ex called them) a more "artsy-fartsy" social circle.

The cracks in our marriage only got worse and the inevitable happened. Separation, then divorce. A part-time position as a bookseller at Barnes & Noble turned into a full-time gig as the Events Coordinator, and everything began to fall into place.

My first "Rockford" poem was about my experience checking out at Logli's, a now extinct grocery chain. Contrasting the slower pace and lack of a sense of urgency against my So. California expectations when doing something as mundane as paying for my groceries was an eye-opener. I was able to give this common interaction with the lotus-eating check-out girl manning the register the slightly twisted and comedic perspective of an outsider. I wrote about waiting for a poetry reading to start at the now defunct Cannova's Italian restaurant (on Riverside just east of the Rock River,) and having a startling epiphany in the men's room. My poem about drinking shots of tequila and getting buzzed while on a date at the Alvarez restaurant on Bell School Rd. turned into a metaphor about one of the greatest comebacks in the sport of boxing by the great Julio César Chávez. Walking home from a downtown job during a cold winter afternoon, I approached Beatty Park just as a wind kicked up. Suddenly I was in the middle of a swirling and chaotic cloud of snow dust sparkling in the late afternoon sun, causing me to pause and take notice of the beauty engulfing me in that moment. Another time I was sitting in one of my favorite watering holes (Bacchus), drinking away the pain of being rejected by a woman as the tv over the bar was showing a formula one race. I was mindlessly watching for the distraction it provided from the throbbing hurt sitting in my chest. Suddenly it came to me; I asked the bartender for a piece of paper and wrote the draft of a poem about how surviving a race crash must be like walking away from a breakup. I could feel myself begin to pick up the broken pieces and become whole again.

Women and drinking became a frequent theme because the women in Rockford are mysterious, intelligent, resourceful, bewitching, and beautiful creatures. They have made me laugh and cry, and everything else in-between. They broke my heart many times, and I'm sure I broke a few myself, but I always came back for more. I wrote about them while having a few beers at C.J.'s or watching them go in and out of the apartment building on N. Main, (across the street from the University Club,) or when having my hair cut by Karla, the woman who knew me all too well. I lived at seven different addresses from 1995-2002, and one of them was a roach-infested building, my apartment just above the dumpsters in the alley. During the summer their contents would cook and reek as roaches on the walls watched me pound my keyboard, writing about the hooker who lived on a different floor and how, upon returning home after a hard night on the job, she would wake me up at three a.m. as she called out from the alley, asking a friend to come down and unlock the entry because she had lost her key. Oh, let me not forget to mention my many nights at the Irish Rose, surrounded by some of the town's most nefarious predators and where my favorite waitress always put a smile on my face. It was a meeting place for angels and demons, the smoking of a late-night cigar, while the Beat Merchants provided the soundtrack all under one roof.

On worst days when I wanted to give up on my writing and felt shitty about life and where it had taken me up to that point, all I had to do was take a walk along the Rock River, sit at my favorite bench, and feel its soothing calm pick up the cloud hanging over my head and carry it away. The bad taste in my mouth would begin to fade, and I could go home in a much better mood. I have a spiritual connection to the Rock, and I make it a point to visit that bench whenever I return to hang out with friends.

Besides poetry, I've included an excerpt from a "creative non-fiction" essay, (MFA speak for "names have been changed to protect the innocent and the truth may be enhanced.") The reader will also find (for lack of a better definition,) the beginning of a "work-in-progress." It's fictional. If you think you see yourself in there... well, maybe you do or maybe you're reading too much into it.

Rockford, what started out as the typical New and Selected has turned into this, The Screw City Poems, my equivalent of a love/hate letter. I honor your beauty, your ugliness, your desire and efforts to rise and be the shining city resting on both sides of your sacred river, and at the same time unable to shake off that festering nest of conservative and anal resistance to social change and progress (can you remember how to say "class action?" C'mon, you 'member!)

You provided what I needed to break the chains keeping me from becoming my true self, and for that I will always be grateful. Meet me at the Polish club for a shot of blackberry brandy and an ice cold PBR. Here's to us, and those like us.

After all is said and done, "It's all about the poem."

Richard Vargas, 7/5/2024

## Part I

"The Establishment encourages poetry to be religious, esoteric, tame —because poetry unleashed is a revolutionary form and is threatening. But Richard Vargas's poems defy such limits that make poetry, even if technically brilliant, boring to anyone but specialists. He is part of the poetic revolution emanating from Long Beach, California, sparked by the remarkable Gerry Locklin, encouraging poetry to be about issues we all care about, both public and private. As Richard demonstrates, these poems work as public performance or read to yourself—they're gripping both ways…" excerpt from Edward Field's foreword to *McLife,* 2005

**it's a living**

it's called customer service
trying to help my fellow man
make sense of the medical insurance
some slick carpetbagging agent
talked him into buying

there are no easy answers
like today
the guy on the phone
was speaking with restraint
holding on to his dignity
but i know begging when i hear it
his voice cracked as he told me
the doctor tending to his dying wife
was getting phone calls from one
of our case managers
being pressured to get her
released from the hospital

please he said
please ask them to stop
she's in so much pain
my wife my best friend
she's in a lot of pain and
there's nothing they can do
please stop the phone calls

i tell him he's got us mixed up
with someone else
there is no record
of any phone calls
in his wife's file
but i know better

i want to put him on hold
go find the sterile room with
white walls where faceless people
hold jelly donuts gripped
tight in their pudgy hands
as they put dollar signs
on the way we die

i want to stick my head inside
remind them that
sooner or later we all
finish the race
sometimes it ain't too pretty
but in the end
if we're lucky
we'll have the love
of a precious few
maybe the ability to stare
death in the eye
so let this one go
just leave her be

but instead i assure
the guy i'll do my best
to find out what's going on
wait for him to hang up
decide to take my break
10 minutes early

times like this i wish
i'd taken up smoking

**laid off**

they hold their heads high
say they saw it coming
(they did) and knew
how to take it in stride
(they didn't)
all week whispered conversations
about unemployment benefits
and maybe going back to school
then the planning out loud for all to hear
about meeting at a local bar Friday after work
to get blasted and let it all hang out

if you were one of the lucky ones
you'll pass because after the 3$^{rd}$ round
weird looks will begin to come your way
the comic book bubbles over their
heads where you can read their thoughts
will say the same thing:
"why not him?"

then you'll blink an eye and see it
reflected back at you in their faces
the shotgun someone will clean tomorrow
and come Monday you're sitting at your
desk taking a phone call
whipping around to see what made
the loud metallic click behind you

you'll blink again
now you're back in the bar
Hank Williams is on the jukebox
they're all lifting their glasses
in your direction

you read someone's lips
as he/she says:
"watch out man,
you could be next."

**for an old teacher, an old friend
(for Gerald Locklin)**

dear Gerry,
so how's it going?
it's been awhile
i hope you sometimes kick back
in your faculty office and wonder
what the hell ever became of me
i kinda dropped out of sight
after my episode in the Long Beach
drunk tank in '79, maybe it scared me off,
but things weren't the same after that
i like to think you knew i'd be back
because after all, i'd tasted good poetry
felt it pour out from my fingertips
and once we're marked by the beast
embrace it...we're doomed for the duration
i remember our attempt to comprehend Finnegan's Wake
(you wanted to read the book, but kept putting it off
so you figured if you taught the class you'd
have to pick it up)
the joy i had getting drunk before noon
and, together, trying to decipher Joyce
at his best was a highlight of my education
or the time i started publishing my poetry mag
and the lead poem was something you wrote
called "I wish they could all be California girls"
the subject matter having to do with fellatio
and the local bronzed babes
the first printer i went to was so disgusted
he refused to accept my order, called my
little mag "filth" and "dirty"
the last time i saw you was in '84
returning to So. California i found myself

asked to give a reading at an art gallery
in Belmont Shore...i was pleased to know
someone still appreciated my work, but Magic
was leading the Lakers against the Boston Celtics
that night, so i agreed to appear with mixed emotions
i knew i had made the wrong decision when
halfway through my set i looked up and saw
some idiot slumped in his chair, sound asleep

then i realized the whole crowd consisted
of wannabes waiting for me to shut up
so they could read their stuff
i wrapped things up early and walked out
with a bad taste in my mouth
found a bar and caught the 2nd half of what
turned out to be a great game
but as i exited i walked right past you
didn't even extend my hand

which brings me to last night
a bunch of us were sharing a few pitchers
at Cannova's
i stumbled to the john
and when i looked in the mirror
it struck me
there i was in my K-mart polo shirt
my baggy khaki pants
my "comfortable" shoes
(and after being out of California for a year
and for once not caring about how i look)
my love handles were blending into
my soft, 41 year old belly
top all this off by my piss poor
attempt at growing facial hair
and the only thing missing are your trademark

Clark Kent glasses
but the kicker was the pee stain between my legs
cause i'd whipped my pecker in too fast
"my God" i said,
"it's him. i'm turning into Gerry."

i can only hope this reads like the compliment
it's supposed to be
and the poetry keeps flowing
for both of us
always...the Kid

## going solo

i practice religiously
always prepared for those
times when i'm by myself
falling asleep waking up
only to wrap my arms around
stale air and nothing else
while the loneliness of the
times i live in cut my insides
like a dull knife

this is when i give in
surrender to my own touch
feel fingertips sending sensations
from synapse to synapse
my body becomes a static
wave of electrical sparks
me a flashing neon sign suspended
over Times Square
my mood determines the style
sometimes quick and powerful
the almost brutal force lifting my
hips off the bed
surging upward into space
or i can pace myself
with the patience of boiling liquid
cresting the rim, receding, cresting
receding until the final overflow
pleasure ripples from the tips
of my hair down to toes
flexed and rigid

some say God calls me a sinner
a man without self-control

i say He knew what he was doing
could see ahead to those times

those humid summer nights
simmering in my personal
solitary hell
when the time it takes
a bead of sweat to slide
down the bridge of my nose
seems like an eternity
and my closest friends might as
well be the stars in the sky

## tequila

drinking it straight
is kinda like climbing
into the ring with
a real pro
one of those Mexican
fighters with a record
of 40 wins by knockout
and two losses by TKO
so the first shot goes
down like liquid fire
but man you
know you're alive
dancing and juking
keeping a safe distance
scoring with jabs
and uppercuts at will
it feels soooo good
you order another
more fire in the gut
forget the lemon and salt
you ain't no sissy
your opponent has a trickle
of blood squirting
from the corner of his eye
the black man
with the silver head of hair
sticking straight up
sitting at ringside is smiling
his toothy grin blinding you
with that timeless flash
of polished gold
hell... you say
this is soooo easy

another please and this shot
is smooth… the fire now
more like a hot kiss
the young woman on the barstool
next to you
is impressed and squeezes your knee
the Mexican boxer begins
to wear down
his breathing telling you
his heart is going to explode
any minute
he's yours for the taking
you order another and another
admiring the amazons
strutting around the ring
holding up the posters
announcing what round it is
knowing you can have
your pick or maybe
all of them… later
then sensing it's time
to finish him off
you decide to go in
for the kill
and suddenly he switches
his stance
you were fighting
a right hander
but now he's a lefty
you walking into
a head shot that lowers
your jaw to the bar
your back to the ropes
he begins to jab
hot pokers of leather

into your ribs
tenderizing you like
one big piece of meat
and while lowering your
arms to protect the body
you hear your date ask
from far far away
"can you still drive..."
feel her hands in your
pockets searching for
the keys as tequila
grins back at you
with scheming
conquistador eyes

## nature poem... for Amy

sitting in the living room on a lazy Sunday
watching NFL playoffs and getting drunk
on mimosas
starting on our third bottle of cheap champagne
we know we're getting deep
when she says the other day she saw
a most peculiar thing
a squirrel scrambled up a tree
with a piece of bread only to be
cornered by a couple of crows
trying to snatch his lunch
when, she says, the squirrel tore
off a chunk of bread and dropped
it to the ground
the crows followed it down
fought amongst themselves
while he ate the rest at his leisure
she talks about how she's never
seen that on any nature show and i say
yeah, but you probably didn't see
the squirrel wipe his defiant
ass with the bread
before he gave it up
a true mammalian response
illustrating why we rule over birds who
still think like the little dinosaurs
that they are
but, she says, crows eat roadkill
and have been known to eat
a stinky furry ass from time to time
so they really weren't bothered
sooner or later that ass belongs to them
anyway, which, if you think about it

kinda makes them the republicans
of the animal kingdom

i pop the cork
realize why drunk English majors
don't write for the Discovery Channel

**throwing up at Grandma's (Loves Park, IL.)**

you never know when
you'll fill the void
find a best friend
where there are none
like the time Dan Swanson
and i were eating a 1 a.m.
breakfast at Grandma's
in Loves Park
he ordered an omelet
i got my usual corn beef hash
three eggs over easy
our waitress was good
had a hard face
like she'd been through
tough times
but she kept the coffee
topped off and fresh
she knew what mattered

while she was stopping by
to check up on us
i began to feel queasy
a bitter taste creeping
up my esophagus
erupting molten lava
dribbled out the corner
of my mouth
to her credit
the waitress just stood there
studying the pool of
pink puke on the yellowed
linoleum as if she could
tell my fortune by

staring at it long enough

i got up and walked
to the restroom
rinsed out my mouth
in the sink
went back to my table
where the hostess
the waitress and
a busboy gathered around
my puddle of vomit
trying to decide
who was gonna clean it up
i took the rag from the hostess
wiped it up myself
gave the waitress a five-dollar bill
swore on the graves of my ancestors
i wasn't drunk
well, not that drunk

finally sitting down
to continue where i'd left off
it dawned on me
Dan had never stopped eating
during the whole mess
wiping his mouth
he took a gulp of java
pulled out a cigarette
asked the waitress
for a book of matches
looked at me as if he'd
missed it all
took a long drag
from his Marlboro
saw how much food

was still on my plate
exhaled a casual
cloud of smoke
held out his
empty cup
for a refill

## waiting in line at Logli's...Rockford, IL.

Oh Logli...oh Logli
your checkout stands manned by the brides
of blue-collar workers
these women who move with the
urgency of junkies high on opium
they make the loathsome lines at the
dept. of motor vehicles
look like an "E" ticket ride
at Disneyland

as i pile my groceries up
on her one square foot of
counter space
my Logli girl intently reads
the recipe for "pork chops surprise"
on the back of my can of
cream of mushroom soup
her languid Logli eyes
speak to me of brats and beer on hot humid
weekends, her cheeks flush with excitement
only when her favorite NASCAR driver
slams another into the wall

is it this
just this

as her Logli breasts sigh
rise and fall like soft loaves of
fresh baked sourdough
i smother myself in dreams of
tractor pulls and this
slow-so-slow pace
here in this Midwest

this holy place
this life
this Logli

## McLife I

he was old
shuffled his feet
to a much slower drum
than the rest of us
looked almost comical
in his teal blue polo shirt
with the trademark golden arches
embroidered on his chest
the baseball cap suited for
pimple faced teenagers was
too big, rested on his ears
and tilted to one side
as he bussed the tables
left littered by single moms
and their undisciplined brats

i was going to say something
like "yo, pops, shouldn't you
be out casting a few on a nice
day like this?" but the look
in his eyes said "don't"
letting me know he had
been let go before his time
screwed out of his pension
while heartless young men
in expensive suits exercised
stock options, downsized for profit
vacationed in Cancun
and pulled his medical insurance
like a rug from under his feet

now, snot nosed kids
who think FDR is a new rap group

shoot him orders, hand him a mop
tonight he'll go home
watch reruns of the Honeymooners
drink Jack Daniels from a pint
dream of winters in Phoenix
and the trigger he's
lost the nerve to pull

## turning into strangers

under the cover
of early morning darkness
i lie on my side
silently watch her gray
outline rise and fall
with the soothing
sounds of her breathing
can smell the stale love
and despair clinging
to the sheets
like last night's
cigarette smoke

a few hours later
the car packed
i give her my key
step outside where
the frigid air of a
Midwest February
slaps me in the face

the glowing embers
between us
once bright
now cold ashes
scattered on the winds
of this endless winter

**divorce me**

she says
her resolve gone
having waited a year
for me to come
to my senses

i can see the danger
in her eyes
because the holidays
are upon us now
that time when people
sit down to eat with
the perfect strangers
collectively called "family"
when empty liquor bottles take
up more and more space
in the local landfills

when loneliness and dread
knock on our door
in the middle of the night
hand us a loaded gun
console us
like the compassionate
neighbors we no longer have

divorce me
she says
pained and hurt
while in the corner of the room
the Christmas decorations
wait to be unpacked

little booby traps
set to explode
in our hands

**karma**

i was a cockroach
once
in another life

i learned to live
in any environment
the cool damp spot
under a cretaceous rock
a crack in the crystallized
dirt floor of an atom
bomb test site
didn't mind the lack of light
did most of my fun stuff
in the dark anyway
learned to relish the flesh
of my own kind in a pinch
but through the ages developed
a diverse set of taste buds

survived famine flood
fire plague and
the ghostly trace of t.v. radiation
beamed from the Home Shopping
Network at 3 a.m. on a Saturday
adapted to ultrasound waves
"super-duper-intensified-guaranteed-
to-kill-me" bug spray and
attractive roach condos
complete with complimentary open bar
suspiciously tainted
happy hour food

would lick the potato chip grease

off your fingers and
daringly nibble
the chunks of steak
stuck between
your teeth when you
fell asleep
with your mouth
open

i was one hell of a cockroach
made sure my DNA
would be carried in a trillion
offspring
had the routine down pat

then i died
came back
a human being

## her first porno

she was watching
her first porno video
so we dropped by for
moral support
it was John Wayne Bobbitt's
version of what happened
on the fateful night
his Mrs. decided to
cut to the root of
their marital problems
we couldn't last
the whole thing

his little limp
dick with a 90 degree
bend where it had
been miraculously
reattached
brought to mind
a baby mud turtle
sunning itself on
a rock
we were laughing
so hard our sides
hurt

so when the
vcr was turned off
we found ourselves
watching the Three
Stooges and the
inevitable came to mind
Moe, Larry, and Curly

in a porno film
Moe picking up
a hammer and saying
"a couple of wise guys, eh?"
and pounding little heads
into submission
or the big
pie throwing scene
bodies covered with
whipped cream
Curly diving in
grinning while licking
some matron's big fat butt
until he realizes the
moaning he is hearing
sounds a lot like Moe
and while he is getting
poked in the eyes
the coppers knock down
the door busting everyone
except the Stooges

who jump through a window
escape running down
the street
weenies flapping in the breeze
like three blind mice

## Oklahoma bombing remains to be buried...

"More than four years after the Oklahoma City bombing, unidentified, fragmentary remains will be buried in a memorial grove of trees at the state Capitol... All 168 victims of the April 19, 1995, bombing that destroyed the Alfred P. Murrah Federal Building were identified, but these small bits of tissue and bone could not be linked to any specific body..." Rockford Register Star – 11/23/99

today the wind swoops
down from a grey sky
blows cold across the river
kicks up the last
of the fallen leaves
the bare branches
of the trees shake
and vibrate like
the bones of the dead

i gather my collection
scales of dried skin
fingernail clippings
strands of my hair
prick myself and milk
my blood
drop by drop
wrap it all
in a white handkerchief
bury it in a hole
by the Rock River
dug with my bare hands
i mix salt in the dirt
so nothing will
ever grow there again
pack the soft clay
with the heel of my boot

i refuse to mark
your death with a tree
a garden or a statue
but instead with this
barren spot of earth
desolate and sterile
a personal tribute

let those of the future
walk by this odd memorial
ponder this lifeless patch
of soil surrounded by
so much life

eventually
someone will say
"it doesn't make sense"
and each time those words
are spoken or thought
one more scream clinging
to the inner walls of
our collective mind
will become silent

until all that remains
is the ringing in our ears

**survival**

my California friends send me pictures
of their new homes in the republican hills
of Orange County
a place where they named the airport
after John Wayne

they tell me things over the phone like:
trading the BMW for a vintage jag
a steal from another desperate sucker
going down for the count
the deep-sea fishing in Cabo San Lucas
is better than ever   cheaper too
thanks to another plunge by the peso
and now that they have a wine cellar
the search is on for the perfect chardonnay
meaning frequent trips to Santa Barbara and beyond
the business sold for big big bucks
and damn the dilemma of what to do
after an early retirement

i want to send them pictures of my new place
poetry books stacked around an army
sleeping bag on the floor
in a room a little larger than O.J.'s jail cell

my response:
a six pack of coronas is the closest
i'll be getting to the border for quite awhile
my 10 yr. old Nissan leaks like the car
Sonny Corleone was driving when they
were both turned into a piece of swiss cheese
i live in a town where public reaction to
Madonna's latest movie makes front page news

and yes
it's snowing    again
i want to cry out
i'm so cold
so alone

but i don't
because not long ago i stood there with them
jostling for my space on the 405 freeway
the perfect tan really meant something
mimosa brunches with cheap caviar
and views of blonde surfers bobbing in
the white foam    the girls golden brown with
skin so tight and smooth a quarter would bounce
10 inches off their firm butt cheeks

but the miles between us
have changed the view
from here
my friends look like lemmings
little fucking lemmings
drawn to the sea

who never see the approaching fall
until just before their brains
go splat

on the rocks below

**5/16/02**
**8 months later**

i served during peacetime
never had to take the point
on a real patrol

but now i know what it's like
to see every crack in the
sidewalk

to study strangers approaching me
from afar and gauge how close
is close enough

i hear barking dogs 3 blocks away
and ask why

in public places i sit facing the door
anticipate the look that says
"i-don't-have-anything-to-lose"
the icy gaze raising up to God
just before the unleashing of hell
on earth

at night i dream
of silver pterodactyls
blinded by the sun
circling for a place
to land

and angels
angels falling from the sky
with singed wings

## Van Gogh's ear

found it in the gutter
downtown Chicago
picked it up
put it in my pocket
now it goes everywhere i go
never leave home without it

the FBI found out
invited me to a
mandatory interview
they consider Vincent subversive
a terrorist of art
but a terrorist
just the same
they gave me crayons
blank paper
told me to draw something
i colored red, white, & blue
planes dropping bombs & food
on poor people
they were convinced
i was a-ok

today i held it close
to my own ear
wanted to hear
what it hears

i listened for a long time
the silence almost
drove me crazy

**what love is... for A.C.**

i need this turmoil
this wild mushroom woman
who stirs up the settled
dust of my life
i need this whirling dervish diva
singing jazz under black
silk nights and dead stars
i need her estrogen sparks
to balance out my moody
testosterone tirades

i need to plug
into this dancing goddess
feel her charge my
mad poet man juices
i need her sharp teeth
biting into my sirloin steak soul
watch red blood drip
from the corner of her mouth
i need to lie down next to
this living landscape
booby trapped with
abandoned mine fields
pitted with the scars
of loves past

i need war and peace
holy visions and raging nightmares
i need her to want me
to despise me
pull me close
push me away

the man was right, love is a
dog from hell, so take it from one
more son of a bitch who knows

once you've had it
like this
you don't want it
any other way

## how it was

imagine you are in a car race
one of those European grand prix
where they go for 24 hrs. straight
½ way through something happens
you sneeze you nod
for just a second
close your eyes at the worst
possible time
then the car is spinning
the centrifugal force pulling
your eyeballs out of their sockets
then rolling into the wall
at 150 mph. and death is
on top of you slipping her tongue
down your throat
the flames licking your suit
ignite a natural reaction
muscles push pull lift
you out and while leaping
through mid-air taking a look
over your shoulder at a wall
of flame brighter than a cop's
flashlight in your face at midnight
you can hear the blisters forming
on the bottoms of your feet
sssssssssssssssssss..............
you hit the ground flat
on your chest    pop up
sprint the fastest 100 yd. dash
ever by a two-legged animal
and while running give thanks
to the god who had the sense to
create survival instincts

that's
how it was

the day
i left you

**for the woman who cuts my hair**

i watch in the mirror
a tiny sparrow hopping from
one side of my nest
to the other
she selects and snips
by instinct
leaving no unruly lock
unturned

been with her for three years
the one relationship i haven't
managed to screw up
realizing it's a good thing
to have at least one woman in my life
i can trust within two feet of me
as she holds a sharp pointed object
in her hands

almost blew it
between appointments i took
a pair of scissors to my annoying bangs
gave myself a little trim
our next time together
she was icy as a scorned lover
acted like she found lipstick on my collar
her suspicions eased only when i 'fessed up
promised not to do it again

she cares about me too
disapproves of my alley cat lifestyle
offers unsolicited advice on behalf
of her many sisters
nudges me to settle down

and get soft around the edges

when i feel sorry for myself
wonder if the relationship fairy
has crossed me off her list
i imagine Carla sitting in her chair
cleaning the implements of her trade
biding her time

until i walk through her door
predictable and consistent
loyal and faithful
coming back like
she knew i would
coming back for more

## altar... for Kathy

like an old non-practicing catholic
who can't give up the rituals
i light sacred candles on my window ledge
improvise prayers whispered to the wind
hope somehow they will find their way to you

the green candle is for the time we stayed up
throughout the night revealing how pain and loneliness
have been our closest companions since who knew when
made us lean and strong in spirit
able to remain distant in crowds
provided the shield we needed to go through life unscathed
realizing we belonged to the same wandering tribe
you took my hand and placed it on your small
delicate breast
said you wanted me to touch you
our defenses dropped almost as quickly
as the clothes hitting the floor
around our happy feet

the blue candle is the purr lodged in your throat
when i would come from behind
plant my kiss between your shoulder blades
slide my thumbs under the elastic of your panties
and slowly pull down while my tongue left
a slow sticky trail along your spine
an amorous snail looking for your sex
one lick at a time

when i light the red one...
ahh, the red one
i see the first night you got up from our bed
tiptoed to the closet and returned with your

black leather belt
begged me to use it
whispered in my ear the thing you wanted me to do
scared but curious i lashed out at your pure unblemished ass
felt the heat of your desire scorch my lips
as i kissed the rising welts crisscrossing your flushed bottom

and this candle
this candle is the day i walked out your door
it was November then
it has been November ever since
other women proving to me (as you knew they would)
it doesn't get any better than what i had with you

now, even during summer's hottest day when heat
rises from blacktop
blurry and rippled with a life of its own
i am cold and barren inside

my heart
a tree
which has lost
all its leaves

## McLife  II

sitting here
eating a couple of
fish sandwiches
imagining a sleepy-eyed clown
by the edge of a lake
his line breaking the glassy surface
at sunrise
but it is most likely
a European fishing fleet using those
new-fangled nets that drift
with the currents and kill
all fish big and small
i'm feeling guilty now
but not enough to stop eating
arriving like clockwork
the single parents towing
kids behind line them up
looking like the birds on early summer
mornings combing the lawns
blackholes wide
chirp chirp chirp chirp
stuffing happy meals down tiny throats
happy parent happy kid happy plastic toy
made in a third world country
by a kid younger than the one
now playing with it
driving daddy's new red buick
three teenage babes walk in dressed
in blue collar chic
through the smell of hot grease
and burning meat i sniff the deodorant
they use
the scent of the perfume they got for christmas

the fruity sweet lip gloss on their
full pink lips
the soap they showered in this morning
an old woman who could be
their grandmother is working
cleaning the windows
this old woman who once had
a great pair of gams and danced
to devil music by cats named Basie,
Duke, and Miller as she
fought off the octopus
hands of her drunk dates
sweaty and stinking of beer and smoke

the black kids arriving at the
start of their shift
frying the fries
flipping the patties
spreading the buns
making an honest dollar
trying to make it to their
eighteenth birthday

this is where America eats
where we fill our bellies
and stuff our cheeks
here  here  here
at McDonald's
the feeding trough
of this all consuming
nation

**for Emily, my waitress at the Irish Rose**

who
floats through the room
soft as a cloud of smoke
from a french cigarette
juggles glasses of house merlot
with mystical grace
this bad girl angel
in leather studded collar
comes to me in fishnet dreams
gives me glimpses of billowy
cleavage while she hovers
over my table
her red chile pepper lips glisten
in the soft light of the room
as recorded jazz
starts her round hips to slowly
shift left then roll right
the wiggle in her walk
makes me forget what
i'm supposed to be eating
then she comes close
leans down
her sultry voice whispering
in my ear
"tip me...
tip...
me...
big..."

i'm a ruined man
as my wallet
spreads open
quicker and wider

than the parting
of the Red Sea

**leaving Rockford**

it happened without warning
one day i woke up
sniffed the scent of decay
felt a cold damp worm
burrowing into my bones
watched my poems
fall to the ground
dried up and lifeless

loaded my belongings
into the back of a u-haul
left at dusk like an NFL owner
sneaking out of town
headed for the interstate
caught the nearest on-ramp
submitted to the magnetic pull
between earth and moon
studied the stars like a
AAA road map

finally understood how
Cortés felt the day he
torched his ships
watched them sink
into the sea

then marched desperate
and blind towards
the new world
with nothing left
to lose

## Genesis... Beatty Park

walking home from work
after two days of snow
the streetlamps were
on because it was dark
and up ahead by the park

with the sacred Indian mounds
under the artificial light
the wind had created a
swirling cloud of snow dust
icy electrons circling
in the chaos of creation

knowing an epiphany
when i see one
i approached it
marveled at the work
of a pure artist
stood there in the midst
of infant stars
and the birth
of another cosmos

## McLife III

i'm sitting in the corner
eating my Big Mac and reading the paper
when some of the old people
from the senior citizen rest home
across the street start to arrive
for after dinner coffee and conversation
the workers know all of them
on a first name basis
even let them carry in their own dessert
they talk about who was taken
to the hospital and who just got back
death isn't mentioned but is just around
the corner like that burger pushing clown
whose picture hangs in the lobby
then this one little silver headed lady
in her best polyester pant suit
her rouge-colored cheekbones
making her look like
the grim reaper in drag
jumps up and starts to do the charleston
she dances up to the counter
the people standing in line smile and clap
she dances for the cop drinking a coke
and doing his paperwork
she dances for the guy sitting alone
and talking to himself
she dances for all of us
until she sits back down
her tiny heart clinching
like a tight fist in her chest
daring someone
anyone to show her
that goddamned light

we're all supposed to see
near the end

after awhile
she gets up
crosses the street
chalks up one more day

**not in the job description**

one.
his name was Joe
everybody's favorite
homeless guy
would park his ass
on a soft cushy chair
by the art books for
10 hours or more
sleeping and reading
drinking complimentary
ice water laced with
a slice of lemon
from the café

always had a Salvation Army
sandwich in his pocket
½ for lunch, ½ for dinner
impressed everyone with
his ability to shoot the shit
on any subject
rumor had it he used
to be a high paid engineer
for a company in town
that made parts for
the space shuttle

he liked to take off his
ratty reeboks and put his feet up
on a coffee table airing out his dogs
wearing socks he had not changed in over
a week or more

no one had the guts

to enforce bookstore policy
regarding the wearing
of shoes on the premises
so when some of the booksellers
sought me out and complained
i approached the guy and
told him he had to keep
his shoes on but he made it
personal and accused this
single brown male
making only 17 grand a year
and living in a white bread town
of being prejudiced
which he emphasized
with a single digit salute

i had to back away
knowing i was walking
into a PC mine field
let the store manager
handle this one

two.
besides
it was time for my lunch break
i got a cup of hot water
from the café for my single
Wyler's bouillon cube
and with my free hand
grabbed as many crackers
as i possibly could
while the barista looked
the other way

sat on a stool surrounded

by piles of books
in a quiet corner of
the stock room

crumpled saltines
into my poor man's
chicken broth
sipped and tried
not to think of how
a really good cheeseburger
would taste right now
tightened my belt
counted the days
until the next paycheck
told my co-workers
i was on a diet

they understood

## Part II

"In this collection, Richard Vargas captures the complex relationships of the everyman, creating vignettes that make them larger-than-life, at least for the blink of an eye. Vargas has a keen understanding of simple lives wrought with everyday despair, and his work conveys this with caring, honesty, and humor..." from Nila Northsun's blurb for *American Jesus*, 2007

## 9 Men, 25 Women, 14 Children, One Infant

it's the day after Jesus' birthday
the devout have come to see
how much they can save on marked
down Christmas cards and wrapping paper
these post-holiday locusts looking
for the crumbs they missed

the picture in today's
paper shows the coffins lined up
mourners in the Chiapas sun
beating their breasts
9 men, 25 women, 14 children, one infant
greeted with bullets and machetes on their
way to worship a complacent god

"how much are these cards with the discount?"
but i don't answer
ignore this American cow
with too much makeup and a cheap dye job
instead i hear the sound of a mountain
breeze rustling trees
or is it the wheeze of a sucking
chest wound

"i need to exchange this, do i have
to get in that long line?"
no you don't
you can come with me and walk along
this stream of fresh water
cool and crisp
ponder its bubbling song
washing over ancient rocks
or is that wet noise

a child choking on its own blood

"how long is this sale going to last?"
as long as human lives
can be bought and sold
traded and smuggled
stomped on and swept under the rug
in a world where precious metals
and shiny rocks outweigh your worth
or mine

finally i answer feeling the tears
forming in the corners of my eyes
"these cards were originally priced at $10.50,
and with the sale price you save $5.25."
the customer is happy
corporate is happy
America is happy
everyone is happy except

9 men, 25 women, 14 children,
and one infant

**"it's so easy to be a poet/and so hard to be/a man"**
...from *40,000 flies* - Charles Bukowksi

late Sunday night
i knew i was in trouble when my ex called
loud sad Mexican songs and drunk people
yelling in the background
i can smell the Cuervo on her
breath from 1300 miles away
before i can say hello
she jabs the word "asshole"
into my gut like a hot switchblade
she's just buried her father
and i know from personal experience
how a death can peel back the skin
expose those forgotten scars
and festering wounds from
another time and place

her words flew by like dirty panties
packed with rocks
i heard it all
self-centered/selfish/righteous
uncaring/indignant/shameless
ungrateful/sonuvabitch

it's been awhile since i've had
the mirror held this close to my face
and i'll be the first to agree we
all need this from time to time

i almost hang up but tell
myself to be quiet and listen
it's gonna be a late night
Monday morning is going

to be a bitch

but for now just
say i'm sorry
and mean it

## The Women at C.J.'s

it's always a sobering thought
to realize the music i listened to
when i was a punk doesn't even
qualify as oldie-but-goodie
but is more like Jurassic park

i'm thinking about leaving
going to another bar with
a kick ass jukebox instead
of a cover band singing
"Like a Rolling Stone" while
high on Geritol and shots
of rot gut tequila

when i see them sitting
on the other side of the bar
two middle aged women
one in a pink sweater
hair short and sassy
the type i'd eventually
ask to go steady
sitting with her blonde
cheerleader friend who
wore tight skirts in class
and jumped in the backseat
at the drive-in without
being asked twice

but it's different now
they're hard and lean
bitter around the eyes
maybe a son in college who
has decided to chuck pre-law

and become a poet
maybe a daughter in high
school on the pill
maybe 2 or 3 divorces
to my one

glancing my way
i feel their search through
the pockets of my soul
looking for what i've got to
bring to the table
i feel violated
like having my underwear
drawer ransacked

it's all too much
i decide to down my beer
and make my exit

then Miss Pink Sweater
unwraps a piece
of juicy fruit
pops it into
her pretty mouth
begins chewing the impatient
chew i've seen a
thousand times since jr. high
the chew that says
"you gonna sit there all night
talking to yourself?"

and just like that
nothing else
matters

## On the Outside

it's a mystery to me
how i have so little
in common with my generation
no kids to put through college
no nest egg padded with soft
dreams of condos in Florida
or rustic cabins hidden deep in
the Wisconsin woods

they collect hot stocks
acquire their paper wealth
while i seek out books of poetry
search used CD stores for
vintage jazz classics
they talk about the state of
their current marriage
define themselves around soccer
schedules and seeing the latest
Disney flick

watching them become their parents
i can't help but feel i screwed up
took a left when i should have taken a right
fated to always be on
the perimeter feeling awkward
and undeveloped

but nights when i'm up 'til the wee
hours chasing the perfect poem
can feel its steamy heat brush my cheek
or when i wake up beside a beautiful woman
her gentle snore music to my ears

then it all makes sense and
i give praise to the gods
who took a liking to me
singled me out
pointed me in the direction
i was meant to take

**Truer Words...**

i'm at the Sports Page
on a Friday night
cutting loose with
some co-workers
find the nerve to break
the ice with a curvy blonde
smelling like Winston Lights
and Budweiser
she declines a dance
because she's been moving
all day into her new place
says it took a
lot out of her

but it looks promising
so before i offer to buy
a round i go to the john
with thoughts of
maybe
possible
why not
and while standing
in front of the urinal
i look up and read these
words written on the wall
at exactly eye level
as if they had been put there
just for me to see at this
crucial moment in my life:

"no matter how beautiful
she is
someone

somewhere is
sick and tired
of her shit"

pulling up my zipper
i wash my hands
head back into the crowd
remember how the gods
work and why

**Driving to O'Hare**

both are in the backseat
my mother-in-law and her comadre
going back to California for a funeral
it was kind of like Driving Miss Daisy times two
but this is my good deed for the month
and i feel alright about it
they have their rituals
while behind the driver's wheel i hear the unsnapping
of wallets, the sound of unfolding plastic
as they bring out their pictures
play each one like a card in a game of poker
"this is Lori, Sandy's daughter, she graduated from...
she is a... she makes x amount a year... her husband
is going to teach... they bought a new house."
"how nice... she looks like Sandy... this is Chuckie... Tommy's
oldest... he owns a construction company... he built me a new
kitchen.... these are his kids... this one gets all As."
they do this for quite awhile until they realize
they've both been around long enough not to be
able to outdo the other
they begin to talk about the good old days
mom worked in the factory that made uniforms
for the soldiers who fought WWII
her friend worked where they made ammunition cases
mom joined the army and would stand on the runway
giving hand signals to the pilots
helping them park their planes
her friend worked in a foundry making parts for tanks
mom was a real live Rosie the Riveter
driving fasteners into the wings of brand-new airplanes

finally they begin to laugh
both agreeing it's been one hell of a ride

but well worth it
and i take a look in the rearview mirror
humbled by my precious cargo

## Driving to Platteville

he's over 70 yrs old
and we're going to Platteville
the Bears are scrimmaging the Browns
and i know he's getting cabin fever
so when i call him up and invite him
he jumps
we leave early, the morning fog clinging to
everything around us
and he's talking, pointing out back roads
he's explored in his prime with some of the
local farmers' daughters
"there used to be a factory there"
or "they make good cheese here"
he talks of his wife who is always in a hurry
to get somewhere, while he likes to take
his time, wander up the hidden alley or drive
down the nameless road
(now i know why he grins when she tells
everyone who will listen how he constantly
gets lost)
i hear about WWII, a young sailor holding his dead buddy
in disbelief in the middle of battle, and docking
in South America and instead of hitting the local
cantinas and whorehouses he went deep into the
jungle and found a watering hole where he tasted
the native brew
(i imagine him now at the VFW, laughing with his
friends and spending his pension freely, buying
drinks and tipping big)
he talks of waking up the day after his mother died
when he was only seven and finding another woman
in his father's bed
he left, ran away on the trains, rode them from Texas

to Louisiana, then north to Freeport, Illinois
some people took him in, raised him like one of their own

approaching a slight incline up ahead
he points, "i used to make friends with
the illegals that the farmers used to hire
and i would bring them to the top of this hill
and show them the view," and sure enough
as we crest the hill i take in scenery fit for postcards
the lush green of the growing corn
covering the rolling hills flushes my cheeks
i roll down the window and smell the scent of cows
and the approaching afternoon storm
i can only imagine the awe of those men
from Mexico seeing land so fertile all they had
to do was throw the seed in the air and it would
grow wherever it landed

so today i thank you, Armando
for adding me to the list of men you saw fit
to share your view
gracias viejo
mi amigo

# Part III

"It's the small miracles that bear the most light, allow dignity. Each of these poems is like a friend you can kick back with and talk religion, politics, sex, anything you are not supposed to speak of in polite company, and it will be alright. Each of these poems is a light. Some are irreverent and rowdy, and others bear reverence to the earth and sky. They party together. *Muchas gracias*, Richard Vargas, for the miracle of this collection." Blurb provided for *Guernica, revisited*, (Press 53, 2014.)—Joy Harjo, three-term U.S. Poet Laureate

## a sin to remember

sixty miles away from her home
making love on the sly at
the Holiday Inn with a
view of the interstate

i find and kiss secret places
she forgot existed
neglected so long they
bloom from my touch
like desert flowers in the rain
after a hundred-year drought

when suddenly
sunlight from ninety-three million
miles away comes through a
thin parting between the curtains
lands on the diamond ring
she took off and placed
on the nightstand

the room explodes into
a flash of celestial fire
scorched by the heavens
and the heat of our desire

**smoking outside in the alley at 3 a.m.**

she yells the name of a friend
to come down and let her in
a cat locked out of the house
she calls out over and over
as the tired sound of her voice
bounces off walls of stone and
concrete then fades into a
summer night air clinging
to everything like syrup

i get up and look out
my second-floor window
see bright tip of her
lit cigarette glowing
in the shadows
i imagine the faint scent
of lime and rum
the grease stained tens
and twenties stuffed
in her crevices and cracks
her limp dirty blonde
hair tangled in sweat
and Friday night cum

looking up
she sees me
looking down

she blows angry smoke into the air
asks "what the fuck is your problem?"

i gaze long at my
thrift store Barbie

knowing whatever i say
will be the wrong answer

**i have Sandra's boots**

the pair she wears on the original
cover of *My Wicked Wicked Ways*

bloody red lips shape into her
the-world-is-my-oyster smile

black spaghetti strap dress
pulls up high over crossed legs

an almost empty glass of merlot
stands at her dainty booted feet

boots with white stitching
criss-crossing Mexican black
leather like intricate tattoos on a
one-eyed bartender's bicep

boots that i can hear
crunching the gravel
and broken glass in
the parking lot of
a Texas cantina at
3 a.m. on a Sunday
morning and a woman's
firm *nalgas* pressing
against the door of
a rusty sky-blue Chevy
pickup while the taste
of her tequila soaked
tongue tickles the
back of my throat

boots that will kick

my ass to hell and back

and make me whisper
"more"

**why my ex-wife will go to heaven**

one day you find yourself managing
a Hallmark gift shop in the San Bernardino
mall and it's busy because one of the major
holidays is approaching
those ones that bring in the big bucks
that make or break the quarterly profit report
the report that keeps the home office happy
or gives them the excuse to ride your ass into
the ground for the next three months
so this is what it comes down to
as your crew of underpaid clerks
man the register and cruise the aisles
helping customers locate that special piece
of made-in-China merchandise with a
sappy card to match

and as you take position up front to
meet and greet the crowd you notice
the young mother with her toddler in hand
you know the type well
she'll browse and take her time while
junior is turned loose to make like
a Tasmanian devil touching and grabbing
his heart's desire as your staff is transformed
into a team of impromptu babysitters
this is how it is and you accept it

a few minutes go by and you see
the child again as he is leaving the store
but this time someone else is holding his hand
someone avoiding eye contact
someone trying to walk fast and not be noticed

years later you take stock of life's ups and downs
while sitting in a bar in Rockford, Illinois, stacking
achievements and accomplishments against the failures
and the near-misses
wonder what the hell went wrong

always remember this:
how you didn't hesitate to approach them
as they attempted to leave
how you ignored the man at his side and
bent down so you looked the kid eye to eye
and asked, "where's your mommy?"
how you heard the sinister whoosh of hot air
as his hand was dropped and the faceless stranger
stepped into the crowd
vanished

later, after reports by security and interviews with police
you took a phone call from the near-hysterical parents
who kept repeating "thank you, God bless you,
thank you, God bless you, thank you, God bless you..."

they were chanting for you
elevating your spirit and
that's as good as it gets

**women and guns**

I.
she says she sleeps with one under her pillow
her daddy bought it for her and they
like to spend Saturday mornings walking
in the woods and shooting at shit
i know where i'm not sleeping tonight

II.
she's new in town
carrying a chip on her shoulder the size of Brooklyn
which also happens to be where she's from
while driving around in her '93 Nissan looking
for a place that's supposed to make a mean falafel
she tells me her gun is in the trunk and it's a good thing
because the way people drive in this town
if it was within reach she'd use it to blow away
the next idiot who cuts her off
i know where i'm not sleeping
ever


III.
i'm talking to my ex on the phone
about the crazy women i've been meeting lately
and she says (half joking half serious)
hell, it's good for you i didn't have one
when we were breaking up because i sure
would have used it

i hang up feeling like my luck
is about to run out

## wedding poem for Lily and Chris

so this is what it's come down to
after the invites are mailed and
the colors are picked and the brides-
maids cringe at the dresses they
have to wear but with the understanding
the only one that counts is the bride
as she walks down the aisle classy
like a Princess Diana with just a touch
of sultry Marilyn Monroe

the groom basically shows up
in his rented tux and shiny black shoes
tries to stay loose and not keel
over which sometimes is the
most important job of the day
love is pledged and "I do" is said
then a kiss to seal the deal
to loud and approving applause

it's on to the reception as spoons
tap on glasses and the couple's
first dance ever as Mr. and Mrs.
the cake is cut and bets are made
will they be civil about it or shove it
down each other's throat
the bride shows some leg as
the garter is slid down her shapely
calf and the single men jostle for
position like basketball players
during an inbound pass
then the ladies take the floor
leaping into the air like NFL
receivers making an end zone catch

coming down with the bouquet
doing the "I'm next" victory dance
later the DJ plays *"Respect"*
and *"What I Like About You"*
as everyone on the dance floor
is laughing and sweating because
today is for being happy

being happy with the hope that
man and woman can still share
their dreams and stand together
against the odds while making it in
a world that gets crazier
every time we turn on the
evening news

so tonight when we lie down in
our beds the joy we witnessed today
will take root and tomorrow
blossom with the realization

that maybe
just maybe
there is still enough love
left in this big whirling
ball of dysfunction
to go around
for the rest of us

# Part IV

"Here is a collection of poems fit for a person's last meal. It does not ask for anything in return, knowing that our collective journey is in that final moment when we share the same language. Richard Vargas's poetry captures life's beauty, absurdities, and the memories almost left behind. These are poems that rise above the *joda*, the struggles of everyday life only a poet of his caliber can muster with eloquence and fortitude." Blurb for *How A Civilization Begins,* (Mouthfeel Press 2022.)
—Levi Romero, Inaugural New Mexico Poet Laureate

**what would Buk do?**

in bed she says she's going to leave
wishes she hadn't come over
feels unwanted

hindsight says i was supposed to
beg and plead for her to stay
but i'm thinking of the beer
and wine she's been drinking
since she got here when i ask
"baby, can you drive O.K.?"

she swings her legs over the side
sits up and spits out "fuck you"
then gets dressed and packs up
all her shit

her black border collie
the coolest dog i ever met
gives me her "what are you
gonna do?" look as she follows
her to their red Nissan

i stand on the front steps
in my robe watching her load
the car and slamming
the door as she gets in
and starts the engine

turning out the lights
i go back to bed
a night breeze comes
thru the open window
i hang a leg out from

under the sheet

it is cool and
feels good

**1958 Vintage Valentine's Day Cards at the Antiques Roadshow**

this is a set of vintage Valentine
cards from the 1950s
the kind of cards kids' moms
would buy them to be passed out
to their classmates on Valentine's Day
nowadays they all have themes
based on the latest superhero
or Pixar movie
but back then they were more
colorful and corny
coming in various sizes
biggest (i really really like you)
to miniscule (i have no idea who you are)

they were manufactured
by the JDL Press Co. in
Dinkford, Illinois, which was
started and owned by the late
Joseph "Dinky" Lundgren
in 1910 who made a fortune
printing pulp fiction paperbacks
never mind the inks they used
were highly toxic and what they did
to the Dinkford River caused it
to catch fire in the infamous
River of Flame incident of 1934
that one cost Dinky almost all
the family fortune in political bribes
to keep him out of prison
and after it was all said and done
he turned the company over to
his sons and retired broken in spirit
and almost in wallet

the greeting card business
became a sideline that
took off when America
realized creating holidays
obligated people to spend
money on useless crap
in order to prove such
things as their love for
a spouse or parent
and their loyalty to
God and country

so the tradition of giving out
Valentine cards was encouraged
and cultivated as a healthy
and wholesome activity for children
of which there were many since
the G.I.s returning from the war
had read Dinky's paperbacks loaded
with big-bosomed dames
and innuendo while holed up
in foxholes and flying bombing
missions and they came home
chomping at the bit and ready
for the real thing

so there were a lot of kids
and money to be made
then and for years to come

now, introducing Valentine's Day
in the schools created a lot of stress
for the children back then
who usually had an idea

who would get the biggest
and mushiest card
it was their opportunity
to let that special boy or girl
know how much they
had the hots for them
even if they didn't know
what the hots meant

but that was the easy part
because once you designated
who would receive the biggest
card in the set
you had to decide who
would get the other biggest card
(there were always two)
and this required a lot of thought
you didn't want anyone getting
the wrong idea or creating confusion
in the mind of your true love
it had to be a safe selection
and as we all know now
when it comes to the affairs of the heart
being safe makes for the kind
of dull days that can lead to
a lifetime obsession with animal porn
or being tied up and peed on

it got even more complicated
since all the cards are geared
to a "will you be mine" mentality
which is a hard thing to give
to your friends of same gender
little boys especially had
a hard time with this

even if you had "special" feelings
about some of your pals
you didn't want your best friend
in that kind of way
you just wanted to say thanks
for the new cuss words he
shared with you and how much
fun it was frying ants
with his magnifying glass
during recess

but now you had to hint at
a degree of want and implied lust
that included him and you and it was all
a complex uncomfortable mess
but the most dreaded part
was receiving a big Valentine card
from the ugly kid everyone avoided
at all costs or went out of their way
to tease and humiliate
or the creepy kid that wore the same
clothes day after day and would go
behind his favorite tree on the playground
and stay there until it was time to go back to class
that meant all along
when you imagined them
checking you out from across the room
well, they actually were
the next few days were spent
plotting how to turn that around
real quick
your reputation and standing
in the pecking order was at stake

thank you for bringing this in today

these cards are a true part of Americana
representing an age of innocence
and purity from which the country
never recovered

## Desiree's poem... Surf Lounge, 1996

i promised i'd write her a poem
a woman who could make
men do the stupid things
like start wars or beat up
their best friend
but all i can think of
is that king in the bible
who wasn't going to kill
John the Baptist until
Salome did her dance
on his lap and squirmed
down hard as she
nibbled his ear

her dark soft hair teasing
his flabby chest as bloodshot
eyes rolled back and he
whispered "yes...yes...
yes!"

her price met
before he even knew
what it was

**what love is #2**
**("I love you too, but not in that way…")**

no sooner had the words
left her lips when
the sound system in the café
begins to churn out
the opening notes
to Bob Marley's "Waiting in Vain"
the bittersweet sound
of his voice coming to terms
with what will never be
while the flame in his heart
refuses to be snuffed out
makes my insides sink
down into the chasm
unfolding before me

wise men and women
throughout the ages
have told us the universe
is ruled by love
maybe
maybe not
all i know
is right now

on any given day
love can be
one cruel and cold
mother fucker

**November 2016**
**doing laundry the saturday after the election**

wondering if the numbing sensation
i wear these days like a second skin
will ever slough off
will i ever feel again

when on cue
as if she could read my thoughts
a stout and voluptuous black woman
standing at the table behind me
breaks out into song while folding
garments of all sizes from the several
piles of clothes rising before her

her sultry voice honed from a people's history
hanging from the wrong end of a rope
sings of being a motherless child
needing guidance from heaven
and a strong shoulder to lean on
during the dark days ahead

so it happens here
in the most unexpected of places
gospel and blues wrapping around
the cold dead space in my chest
transforming it into a warm shelter
for my anger to lie down and sleep

this is the part of the poem
where i'm supposed to praise
our ability to take a hard sucker punch
and carry on the good fight
but the reality is this pool

of sewage and shit we made
for ourselves is sucking me down
i'm choking on tears
yet to be formed

the words on the page of the book
i hold in my hands begin to blur
and slide off the paper

i pretend to continue reading

**thanksgiving; a rebirth**

no family meal
no friends and drink
laughter or lounging listless
on soft sofa watching meaningless
football games

i walked to the edge of the Rock River
lit dried sage bundled and wrapped
in scarlet twine

faced south as smoke
encircled me under gray sky
and cold air embraced my bones
closed my eyes and prayed
asked that my brothers and sisters
protecting our water and lands
be safe from rubber bullets and grenades
water cannons and tear gas
asked the spirit of the river
to come between them and
the corporate enforcer's intent

faced west and felt the sacred smoke
wash over me as i asked for strength
of heart and resolve of spirit to face the rising evil before us
to be worthy of the pain that awaits in the days ahead
asked for a shield of butterfly wings and a sword of feathers
arrows made of poems and song
sharp and straight

turned and faced north
thoughts and prayers sent to
comrades in arms

fellow veterans deploying to meet
the serpent of greed head on
plunging into combat with
the will of the warrior and the
heart of the peacemaker

finally i faced the east
grateful for this moment
my renewal of self
as i inhaled the surrounding smoke
and felt one with the calm
flow of the river
embracing me
bonding me to this land
and its people

i dropped the burning sage
my gratitude acknowledged
by the soft sound of water
meeting flame

## Part V

"Richard Vargas writes about work, play, survival, the grief and joy of inhabiting this world of ours in language that is direct, enthralling, and sagacious. This terrifically crafted collection finely counterpoises light and dark and is a testament to the poet's compassion and empathy." Blurb for *leaving a tip at the Blue Moon Motel,* (Casa Urraca Press, 2023.) —Richard Modiano, Director Emeritus, Beyond Baroque Literary/ Arts Center

**the time traveler's advice**

i visit me at age 60
tell him not to mope about the breakup
the young ones leave sooner or later
i would have done the same
the return to the Midwest is solid
but for the wrong reasons
don't be so quick to whip out
the credit cards and quit drinking
those pricey craft beers
no shame in popping open a PBR

now i sit on the sofa
next to myself on my 50th birthday
in my 1st apartment in Albuquerque
i am tripping on the batch of pot brownies
i baked earlier for the people i invited
to come over and help celebrate

the young couple from the first floor
arrived early and are in the kitchen giggling
they asked me if i'm high and it
took me 10 minutes to answer
i wish myself happy birthday
and leave it at that knowing
the phone call i get from my brother
two days from now will be the last time
i ever talk to him
i want to say "you did your best
the truck crashed
it was his time
don't feel guilty"
but i know it won't
make a difference

at age 40 i sit at the table
in Cannova's with a trio of
young women waiting for
the poetry reading to start upstairs
i watch me order another pitcher
and i can't take my eyes off
one of the women
she has long brown hair
a smile that can make the devil
lay down his pitchfork
and a singing voice
that only gets handed out
when the angels are sending
one of their own to walk among us
i bend over and whisper
in my ear "don't expect anything
to come of this. be grateful for
what she gives you, but know
she will crush your heart."
i turn around as i walk out
and can tell i heard nothing i said
and for my own sake i'm glad

my 30-year-old self
is crumbled on the floor
in the condo i am buying
with my wife who is still at work
i have a cold Corona in my hand
while i weep at the foot of the
christmas tree with the flashing lights
it is my birthday and i always thought
i'd know why my father OD'd at age 29
my 30-year-old self has lived longer than
he did and the answer was supposed

to be there waiting for me

i can only hold myself
whisper in my ear
"the poems will come"

21st birthday
i take a seat next to me
we celebrate alone in a sticky
booth in the back of Li'l Abner's
my first time in a topless bar
a woman with a white cowboy hat
boots and a sparkly blue bikini
is dancing to "Convoy"
i watch me walk to the stage
with a dollar in my hand
she greets me at the edge
let's me tuck the folded bill
wherever i please
bends down and kisses me
on my mouth
our tongues touch
sitting down, i ask my waitress
to break a twenty

i get up and leave me there
eyes fixated on the dancers
"Convoy?" really?

it's my 10th birthday
i watch as my dad gives me
two birthday presents
a set of oil paints and an illustrated *Gulliver's Travels*
stories about a guy who leaves home
and is always on the outside looking in

as if the old man is trying
to tell me something
twenty-four days later he shoots up heroin
in a Compton garage
nods out for the last time
leaving me for good

i am writing this down in my present
the next breath it becomes my past
while the blank space awaiting the words
that follow is the future

i pay attention
look where it got me

## Paydazed (an excerpt)

Two.

During the 1990s, I lived in Rockford, Illinois; one of those small towns that keeps getting listed on the Forbes Magazine list of "lousiest places to live in the U.S." They drink a lot in Rockford. During the winter, the residents form dart leagues and bowling teams so they can meet at a bar and drink. During the summer, they form softball leagues so they can meet after the game and drink. The Rock River splits the town in two. Old houses and most of the black and brown residents on the west side, newer houses and most of the white residents on the east side. Being the hometown of Cheap Trick is Rockford's claim to fame, that and a prominent porn star they don't like to talk about. And yes, places of worship almost match the number of bars and dives, of which there are a multitude.

I was working on the eastside for Blevins & Nubbs Booksellers as their Community Relations Manager. I organized the monthly calendar of store events. My duties included contacting authors for appearances and booking local musicians to play in the café. I started poetry workshops, book clubs and cajoled my fellow employees to put on smelly Cat-in-the-Hat or Clifford costumes (passed around from store to store) for story hour in the kids' books department.

Once, out of curiosity, I converted my salary to an hourly rate. It was barely over eight dollars an hour. Sometimes I hocked my VCR twice in the same month, other times my gold ring. Or I'd get a loan from one of those places that gave advances on my next paycheck. I had to eat. I had to buy gas and pay for dry cleaning. I was making $17,500 a year. When I quit the bookstore for a higher-paying job, they paid me for my unused vacation time. A month later, I got a letter from them; vacation pay was issued in error. Could they please have their money back?

I remember the high arc of the wadded-up request for the return of their vacation check, floating through the air, dropping down into the wastebasket across the room with a *whoosh*. Nothing but net. The crowd went wild.

***

January 1999. My new employer was Konsiko Medical Insurance. The company occupied a couple of buildings downtown. A two-story building with majestic columns and fake Greek architecture, and a tall, multi-storied office building right on the banks of the Rock River. I worked on the third floor in the call center. Rows and rows of desks, phones, computer monitors, keyboards, and headsets. All of us talking at the same time; a cacophony of voices all saying at once, "Hello. Thank you for calling Konsiko Medical Insurance. My name is ____. How may I help you today?" I learned a new language. Co-pay, Deductible, Out-of-Pocket, Pre-existing Condition, PPO, HMO, Primary Care Provider, In-Network, Out-of-Network, Policy Exclusion.

I learned the art of how to say "no" without actually saying it: Your prescription benefit is maxed out for the year, all your prescriptions will now be "out of pocket"…the procedure is "excluded" from coverage…the doctor was "out of network," so you will have a higher "co-pay"…you did not get a "referral" from your "primary care provider", so the office visit to that specialist is not covered…your doctor used an "out of network" lab so your "in-network co-pay" does not apply…your "annual" benefit for chemo has been "depleted" and it won't be covered again until next year…the address for appeals is…

Sometimes the person on the other end of the line erupted in a burst of anger and name-calling; other times they broke down and cried. I preferred the name-calling.

The Konsiko Medical Insurance company magazine liked to feature articles about the tropical resort reserved for their sales team's elite performers: ringed with white-sand beaches, a turquoise-blue ocean, and a pool with a bar you could swim up to. Beautiful people were seated at the bar, sipping decadent drinks decorated with colorful little paper umbrellas. Everyone was laughing and having a great time with their glowing tans, washboard abs, wet and sexy swimsuits, and perfectly straight white teeth. Contrast this with the call center's morale boosters: "blue jean" Fridays when the dress code was relaxed and we were allowed to wear comfortable clothes for eight hours. Or the monthly potluck: crock pots of all shapes and sizes lined up in the break room emitting the aroma of cocktail weenies cooking in their "special" sauces, sloppy joe hamburger meat, store-bought buckets of potato and macaroni salads, and one of those huge sheet cakes from the local supermarket covered in a thick sugary frosting that dissolved tooth enamel after three bites.

We were the belly of the beast.

***

When the company's plan to expand by acquiring the nation's largest mobile home lender backfired, Konsiko's stock went from thirty-five dollars a share to (literally) a handful of pennies. Every day I reported for work was like reliving all the desperation and anxiety of the last hours of the Titanic. They announced they would be laying off a few of us at a time, every month, until we were all gone. I volunteered to be one of the first. Upon receiving my severance check, I rushed to the bank to make sure it was good.

And the CEO who ran the operation into the ground? I imagine his well-planned exit, the perfect timing of a pilot ejecting from his plane just before the crash, saving his own ass, his golden parachute landing him gently at poolside, where he promptly found a seat at the bar and ordered a mango-pineapple-banana-passion fruit margarita.

## Part VI
## A Work in Progress

one.

Dinkford, Illinois. A small town split right in the middle by the Wish-eewaukee River. A little-known fact: many of the old timers were always proud to enlighten newcomers that Dinkford once had a place on Hitler's wish list of places to bomb in the U.S., because it was a manufacturing hub that made eighty-nine percent of the screws and fasteners used to hold together the nation's arsenal during WWII. Thus, the nickname "Screw City."

Another little-known fact, but much more hush-hush, was that Dinkford, approximately 70 miles north of Chicago, was long ago deemed a mafia neutral territory, i.e., mobsters could retire there, from any gang or family, and live out their golden years without fear of retribution for their sins of yesteryear. One of the more exclusive homes along the west bank of the Wisheewaukee was built by Al Capone. He used to go there to relax with his dames and cronies. On warm summer days they played croquet on the manicured green lawn alongside the river, betting a hundred bucks a ball, just to keep things interesting. Rumor had it that he made the best lemonade in the city.

When I arrived there in the summer of 1995, fresh out of college, having just accepted a junior management position with a medical insurance company occupying several floors of the tallest building downtown, Dinkford was in the middle of trying to recover from bad economic times. The downturn of the 1980s had taken a hard toll on manufacturing all across the country, but especially in small union towns like Dinkford. Once a thriving hub of factories and manufacturers, it now found itself drying up as companies flocked to other locales overseas, where the labor was cheaper and profit margins could be expanded.

But Screw City by the river held its chin up. The people loved to play in softball leagues during the summer, and drink. Form dart teams and bowling leagues in the winter, and drink. Play Thursday night bingo at the V.F.W., and drink. Sit down to a Friday night beer battered walleye dinner at the Polish Club, and drink. The locals loved to gather around television screens in bars, or at home, and root for their teams, Da Bulls/Da Bears/Da Cubs, with the lone exception being all the Packer fans in town, (since they were only about 12 miles from the Wisconsin border,) and drink. When Spring came along, the town had outdoor festivals at McKinley Park, under the stars and alongside the dark green waters of the Wisheewaukee, consisting of a stage, local bands or the occasional touring classic rock band, and a row of concession stands hawking butterfly porkchop sandwiches, grilled brats, and cold beer.

And like all little dysfunctional Midwestern towns, Dinkford had as many churches as it did bars and dives. The Italians and the Poles laid claim to the many old Greystone and brick catholic churches spread throughout town. The black side of town was peppered with churches where soulful Sunday morning song and music echoed on every other street corner. Lutheran and Presbyterian churches pitted themselves against the rising competition of modern evangelical super churches making headway in a town that had enough sin to go around for everyone.

After I got situated and became familiar with the lay of the land, I found myself becoming a regular at a quaint, but popular, hangout called the James' Choice. The place was a throwback to a time when the neighborhood drinking establishment had copper tile ceilings, a squeaky wooden floor, sturdy booths, and a big, solid oak bar running the length of the wall. Framed pictures of James Joyce in various poses, drinking and/or writing, were hung without rhyme or reason wherever there was an empty space on a wall. Large windows stretched up to the ceiling creating a wall of glass, which let in the natural light of day, and the eerie artificial downtown light of night. The wall of glass always made me feel like I was in the middle of a huge fishbowl, where the hip, single beauties of downtown would swim from one table to the next, patiently waiting for someone to buy them a drink or offer them a few lines of coke. Customers sitting on the bar stools could see themselves reflected in the large mirrors mounted behind the bar. The bartender was usually a flurry of activity serving from an extensive selection of beers, wines, whiskeys, vodkas, and everything else in-between.

Live music was featured on the weekends, with the occasional art show thrown in. The art shows usually featured the mediocre work of whatever pretty young thing the owner of James' Choice had in his sights at that particular moment. It was during one such night that I first noticed Lina. Or she noticed me.

two.

I was sitting at a table by a window. It was only the second weekend since Penny and I had broken up. It was my fault, mostly. I usually didn't date women with small children, but she was lonely and had only been divorced for about a year. And I was new in town. We had met at a co-worker's Halloween party. My costume that night consisted of red plastic devil horns, a red cape, and a plastic pitchfork. She was the St. Pauley girl, the buxom beer-serving maiden. We hit it off, making jokes throughout the night about me being a horny little devil, and since her kids were spending the weekend with their grandmother, afterwards we found ourselves on her couch, making out until we couldn't stand it anymore. Then she took my hand and led me to her bedroom.

But I wasn't ready to play family man, and her ex was an asshole, sabotaging weekend plans on purpose by not showing up to pick up the kids when it was his turn to spend time with them. Then the kids would cry and she was pissed off and we ended up fighting. So much for a romantic weekend.

After one such scenario too many, she told me that if I was so miserable, to just leave and not come back. Made sense to me, I said, as I grabbed my car keys and walked out.

Now I was sitting in the James' Choice on a Friday night, staring out the window, watching the cars drive up and down State St., and having second thoughts. I filled my mouth with smoke from my cigar, then held my cognac to my lips and blew the smoke into the glass. The pungent cigar smoke combined with the aromatic vapors from the liquor was then inhaled through my nose, as I tilted the glass and sipped.

"Interesting. I've never seen that done before."

The woman was sitting at the next table. She was alone, facing me, smoking a cigarette and drinking a ruby red glass of wine. The lighting in the bar had been muted, but the night lights coming through the window were more than enough for me to be taken back by her beauty. The first thing I noticed was her short, boyish haircut. She wore it parted on the side. Her eyes were dark and penetrating, slightly almond shaped. She wore no eye shadow or eyeliner of any kind, instead relying on her meticulously plucked eyebrows to enhance their allure. The lines of her face were soft around the edges, and her nose was in perfect proportion. She wore a gloss on her kewpie doll lips, but nothing garish or dark to distort their natural pink color. Her white skin was unblemished and looked smooth to the touch. In some ways she reminded me of a young Audrey Hepburn.

"I think I saw it done in a movie, once. Don't ask which one, though."

She took a drag off her cigarette, then put it out in the ashtray on the table. "Don't get the wrong idea. Drinking makes me crave a smoke, but only a puff or two. That's the full extent of my smoking. Are you here for the art show?"

"I didn't know there was one tonight. Are you?"

She looked past me, as if she was looking for someone. "Yeah. The artist is a friend of a friend, and we were going to provide some moral support and show up. We have it on good authority that Tim, the owner, is trying to get down her pants. The creep."

I had to laugh. "Ah, it's one of *those* art shows. I've heard he has a real eye for talent."

"Yeah. He's a real ladies' man. Her art isn't bad, but she's definitely not ready for a showing. This will end up hurting her more than helping."

"Can I make a suggestion? Why don't you join me until your friend arrives, and we can talk over one table, instead of two?"

"Why, sir," she said, lowering her gaze and grinning, "I'm not the kind of girl who gets picked up in a bar…"

"I'm Raymond. Vega. There. Now you know me, it's not like you're accepting a stranger's invitation. And you are…?"

"Catalina Keane. I prefer Lina. And I'll accept your invite, Mr. Vega." Her smile was now warm and friendly.

At that, she stood up, picked up her wine glass, set it on my table, and turned around to get her purse and coat. Lina was wearing a black cashmere sweater with a plunging cowl neck, and one could not help but to notice the two pointed tips of her breasts, trying to burst through the fabric. She was also wearing tight, black leather pants and black, ankle-high stiletto boots. She was that rare combination of the erotic, and the elegant. As she leaned over to gather her things, I became aware of my arousal. I realized something about myself I never knew before… apparently, leather appeals to me.

I stood as she began to seat herself, and for a brief second I felt her eyes examining me, up and down. I felt myself blush as she must have noticed the growing bulge in my jeans. If she did, she didn't let on that anything was amiss.

"To meeting new friends." She held out her glass waiting for me to join her.

I picked up the snifter and lightly clinked it against her glass. "God, I certainly hope so."

We spent the next hour getting to know each other. Lina was a native to the area. She was raised on a farm in one of the neighboring towns. Her parents were killed in a car accident when she was 7. A cold autumn night, pitch black, slick country roads, drunk driver crossing the lane into her parents' sedan. They were both killed instantly. She and her little brother were taken in by a childless aunt who lived in Dinkford with her husband. Lina got straight As in school. Honor society, drama club, first string on the girls' soccer team. She was awarded a scholarship to Dinkford College, graduated with an English degree, and now she lived alone, in an upstairs apartment in a cul-de-sac near the YMCA and within a short distance to the river's walking trails. She taught for one year at one of the local high schools, hated it, and a part-time job turned into a full-time position as the community events manager for the Book Nook, the big chain store on the east side of town. She had a close-knit circle of friends, including some of the local artists, musicians, and even a few of the town's politicians and cops. And they all watched out for her.

I told her my story. Growing up in Compton, California. A father who died when I was ten years old from a heroin overdose. My mother remarrying 2 years later. Her husband was a good father to me and my two sisters. We moved to the drab, but safe suburbs of Cerritos, where I, too, got all As. First string on the varsity football team, student body president, went steady with the head cheerleader. Graduated near the top of my class and went on to graduate with a degree in business from USC. Pioneer Insurance, out of Chicago, along with a few other companies, had recruited me at a job fair the business department held every year for their graduates. I chose a jr. management position with Pioneer because I liked the idea of being close to Chicago and Madison, with the potential to eventually get a position in the Chicago main office. I'd been here almost a year, and outside of work, didn't know very many people.

"And I only smoke a cigar a couple of times a month, at the most. It's usually a celebratory act or one that helps me focus when I'm in deep thought." My cigar was done for the night, and I asked the passing waitress to take away the ashtray I was using.

"Really? Well then, I hope this was an evening for celebration."

"It didn't start out that way, but things have taken a turn for the better." I winked and finished off my cognac. "Is your friend going to be here soon?"

"Good question. Let me give her a call." She pulled out her cell phone. "Sharon? I'm here at the Choice. How long... uh huh. Okay. No, that's alright. I met someone and if he's up for it, we'll go ahead and check out Linda's show. Hope you feel better in the morning. Love you, bye." She put the phone back into the purse.

"She's got the beginnings of a migraine. She left me a message, but I turn my phone off when I'm in public. I hate the annoyance, it's rude. Don't you think?"

"I really don't need one when I go out. And yeah, it can be a rude device in the wrong hands. The other day some jerk at the sandwich shop held up the line while he called someone and read them the menu so he could place their order."

"I hate that!" She started to laugh, then asked if I wanted to check out the art show.

I flagged down the waitress, tried to pay for both of us, but Lina wouldn't hear of it, and after we each paid our separate tabs, off we went, across the street to the little gallery the owner of James' Choice used to lure naïve, young beauties into his lair.

three.

The gallery did not belong to the owner of James' Choice, but it had a room in the back available for one-night shows and events. The bright light and white walls were a glaring contrast to the cavern-like atmosphere we had just left. There were several paintings hanging on the walls, ranging in size. A few were very ambitious, almost as big as a closet door.

Lina saw a group of people milling about in the middle of the room, and she took me by the hand as we walked up to join them. Her hand was cold at first, but after a few seconds, the touch we shared began to generate a warmth that was sensuous. I wanted more. And in a small way, I felt as if Lina was publicly claiming me.

She introduced me to several of her friends. There was Maria, a tall, dark haired Italian beauty. Her last name was familiar, and I recalled seeing it mentioned frequently in the local newspaper. Her family was involved in city politics, and a building housing the family law firm downtown had the name carved in stone, prominently on display. I met Rachel, a free-spirited single mom who had the faint scent of patchouli in her hair and a nose ring. Then there was Dan, the guitarist in a popular band. I had heard them play several times, and they were very good. By their third song, the ladies were usually up and moving to the dance floor. He was also a music teacher at one of the high schools.

We made small talk, and all the time I knew I was being appraised. Lina was fully aware of this. I felt her watching me as they made their subtle probes. Then, she bid them a good night as she took my hand again and led me to the table where we each got a cup of wine.

"Very impressive, Mr. Vega. You didn't flinch once."

"I know how to handle myself," I said, taking a sip from the plastic cup. "Wow. Tim doesn't hold back. Where did he get this wine? From a box?"

Lina started to laugh, covering her mouth with her hand. She swallowed the wine and, shaking her head, led me over to a painting.

"Actually, the guy is a wine snob. We're probably drinking a very moderately priced chardonnay."

"Out of plastic cups?"

"Well, he's also a cheap bastard. Now let's look at some... art?"

We found ourselves standing in front of a painting that looked like something right out of a community college art show. The artist apparently liked Dali and Picasso, with a little bit of O'Keefe, but couldn't make up her mind, so she just mixed them all up on the canvas. It was a piece of crap.

"Your friend did this?" I asked.

"Linda and Sharon took a couple of art classes together. She occasionally shows up at a party or barbeque, but I don't know her like Sharon does. That's her, over there, standing by Tim and talking with the editor of *The Wisheewaukee Herald*."

"Ah, that weekly rag that likes to feature the latest conspiracy theory on their front page?"

"Sounds like you're a fan…"

"I am. Where else can I get free paper to line the bird cage? Well, Linda is cute. And by the way Tim has his arm around her waist, I'd say he's gonna be one happy 'cheap bastard' by tomorrow morning. Money well spent."

"No shit. Sharon will be disappointed that we weren't able to save her."

We moved on to the next painting, then the next. As a courtesy, we stopped before every piece of art hanging on the walls. But after the first three, it was apparent that Linda's art wouldn't be featured again anywhere, anytime, soon.

Lina had been standing close to me all this time. She took my hand, pulled out a pen from her purse, and wrote on my palm. Then she kissed me on the cheek, said she had to go, and left me standing there, with her phone number slightly smudged on my hand, as she headed out the door.

four.

That night, I went home to find a message on my answering machine from St. Pauley Girl. She, too, was having second thoughts. She even left open the door for a booty call, no matter how late I came home. I was going to call her back, until I saw Lina's number on my palm. I wrote it down on the note pad I keep by my phone, and in the process my intent to call my ex-girlfriend vanished in thin air.

I tossed and turned in my bed, making up my mind to call Lina the next day. Then I closed my eyes and drifted off to sleep.

I awoke just before dawn, a raging erection throbbing between my legs. I knew what I had to do, whispering Lina's name as I stroked myself to the kind of powerful release that lifts a man's hips off the mattress, my desire and lust consuming me from head to toe.

five.

The next time I opened my eyes, it was around 10 a.m. Saturday morning usually found me doing the mundane things that a single man must do for himself. After a quick shower, I gathered up my dirty laundry and loaded up the car for a trip to the laundromat. I hate doing laundry, but I was down to my last pair of clean underwear. And while I wasn't above making a trip to Kohl's and buying new skivvies to postpone doing laundry for another week, in this case, most of my wardrobe was in that pile of dirty clothes.

Thoughts of Lina lingered as I loaded up the car with laundry and detergent. At the laundromat I picked up a discarded newspaper from the previous day and skimmed from one section to the next. I came across the weekend events section, and halfway through it found an announcement for a book signing later that evening at the Book Nook. Another local writer had self-published and was going to bless the town with his brilliance. Lina would probably be working the event, and I decided to drop in unexpectedly and say hello. It would serve her right for how she disappeared last night at the art show.

The book signing started at 7 p.m., and I arrived at Book Nook a little after the start time. I walked in, made a beeline for the café, bought a cup of coffee, and wandered towards the back of the store where most events were held. There was an open space with enough room for setting up a small table and about 20 folding chairs. The shelves with art books were on the left, and the literature section was on the right. Seated and reading what sounded like trite and sophomoric poetry, with a pile of his recently self-published collection titled *Sunny Days Make Me Think of You and All the Other Guys You Screwed* stacked on the small table next to him, was a young man wearing a black t-shirt, faded jeans, and a beret. His audience consisted of about eight people, and they made it a point to clap every time he finished reading a poem from the book.

I saw Lina, standing between bookshelves in the literature section, flipping through a book while pretending to pay attention to the reader. She looked more conservative in her work clothes, and I noticed a pair of glasses that she had not worn the previous night when we first met. Bookish and sexy. She wore the look well. I swung around and came up behind her. She hadn't noticed me, so when I leaned in close and whispered, "I'd like to register a complaint with the manager regarding this lame and repulsive attempt at poetry" she whipped around, then upon seeing it was me, giggled and shushed me with a finger to my lips.

"Welcome to my world," she whispered, as she returned her attention to the lousy poet. I picked up a book and flipped through the pages.

"He's got about thirty more minutes, plus his book signing, which apparently is going to be very short, thank God. No reason for you to subject yourself to this. I'll meet you in the café when it's over, okay?"

I smiled back, rolled my eyes, mouthed the words "thank you" and headed off to find a table.

The café was a great place to sit and people-watch, one of my favorite pastimes. Geeky, zit faced teens perused the latest comic books, (I mean graphic novels,) sci-fi, and fantasy books. The college students tried to look sophisticated as they skimmed the pages of art and design magazines and sipped on their "double venti skim milk shaken-not-stirred and topped off with extra whipped cream and chocolate sprinkles" latte. Middle-aged single women hunkered down behind stacks of self-help books telling them why they run with the wolves and men are from Uranus. Watching people in Book Nook was the next best thing to sitting in an airport and observing the rituals of my fellow travelers.

I was contemplating getting another cup of java when Lina sat down in the chair next to me. "Having fun?"

"Just passing the time watching your customers. Is this your usual Saturday night crowd?"

"Pretty much. If we have music in the café, we might draw some new faces and a bigger crowd. It's a slow night. I knew our Kerouac wannabe wasn't going to draw, but I like to support our local writers, even the bad ones. Sooner or later they all come back to buy books."

"Good point. So, are you off?"

"Yes. Got something in mind?"

"Well, the art museum is showing a special screening of Casablanca. Do you like classic movies?"

"Rick and Ilsa? Are you kidding me? Let's go!"

six.

Lina invited me to her place after the movie for a glass of wine and late-night conversation. But before we finished our first glass of merlot, we were locked in an embrace on her sofa that could only lead to the inevitable, as she stood up, and taking my hand, led me to her bed. The moonlight filtered through the curtains, bathing the bedroom of her second-floor apartment with a glow not of this earth. We were entering that stage when everything about "us" was exciting and new, still many nights away from becoming the familiar and comfortable. The time when lovers are drunk with desire and lust, stumbling with abandon towards that sweet unknown. Our clothes dropped to our feet and we fell into each other's arms.

I embraced Lina's lithe figure, letting a free hand follow the furrow of her spine, down to the warm crack of her ass. My fingers traced its smooth divide, then slowly came back up to the small of her back, making circles in the smooth patch of her skin. She squirmed, melded her pelvis against mine as our tongues did a slow dance in her mouth, then mine. Her soft lips broke free, and she gently kissed my chin, the tip of my nose, my eyes.

Our mouths pressed together as I slid my hand down her smooth stomach, then let it linger on her firm hip, until it brushed up against the moist patch of hair between her legs. She quivered as I stroked the swollen cleft, tracing its shape with my fingertip. I teased her clit, the palm of my hand moving up and down against her sensitive button while inserting my finger back and forth into the wet hole convulsing tight around my touch.

I turned my head towards the antique vanity dresser she had placed on the side of her bed. There, reflected in the oval mirror, in that other worldly light, were the two of us, encircled by the incandescence of our lust and desire. We could have been frozen in time and placed in a museum, centuries into the future, where connoisseurs of fine art depicting what love can do to men and women, would be compelled to gaze long upon the same scene I saw reflected back at me. Then, I saw her head turn into the mirror. Now, Lina was watching me watch us. We smiled at each other in the mirror, as I positioned my hips between her spreading legs and she reached down for my hard cock, guiding me into the warmth of her sex…

seven.

Lina and I had been seeing each other for the last four weeks. Thoughts of being with her filled my head throughout the day. I was starting to think of her and I as "us." I was 30 minutes early for our dinner date, seated at our favorite table at James' Choice, where I used the time alone to formulate the words I wanted to say, the feelings I wanted to convey. Things were getting serious.

Because I was lost in thought, I did not see Penny when she walked in. Suddenly, St. Pauley Girl was standing next to my table, waiting to be noticed.

"Penny, hey! You look great. Sorry, I was working something out in my head. How are you?"

She was dressed to kill. A tight and short, strapless, red dress with a leather midriff jacket, (what was it about the women of Dinkford and leather?) and black satin high-heels. Penny's long legs were looking mighty fine, and her long and thick flaming locks of red hair fell loose on her shoulders, suddenly reminding me how good it felt to run my fingers through them after a session of making love.

"I'm good, Ray. I'm meeting my date for a few drinks, then we're going to a concert at the Orpheum. How are things with you?" She took a seat before I could ask her to join me.

"Work is work. My last performance review hinted at a promotion soon, but I'll wait and see. I am seeing someone and she's going to be here any minute. How are the kids?"

The conversation was light and congenial. She had decided not to lie around feeling sorry for herself after our breakup. The kids were good and with their father. She had not mentioned her date tonight, so the ex could not sabotage her plans. I told her the bare minimum about Lina, then asked her about her date.

"Oh, what a sweet guy. And he's loaded! Everyone in town knows him... Kumar Patel. He deals in real estate. He practically owns every other building in town."

Just then, a short, dark man meticulously dressed in an expensive look-ing suit walked in, and Penny wished me lots of luck with Lina, as she joined her date at the bar.

I had heard about this guy. The ladies were wary about him. He was a charmer, throwing his money around, driving a new Mercedes, living in a luxury apartment at the top of the Wisheewaukee Towers overlooking the river. He took pride in having a different woman on his arm as often as possible, always on the lookout for young damsels in distress. He wined them, dined them, and back at his place, convinced them to comply with his many kinky urges and needs, as he declared himself a master of Tantric sex who only wanted to teach his victim spiritual ways to achieve the ultimate orgasm. There were many stories, but getting one of his former dates to talk about it directly was considered rare. The local single women shared what information they could gather and did their best to keep each other out of the claws of Dinkford's number one predator. But it was hard to do when a young woman was down and out and desperate.

My heart sank as they walked out hand in hand and got into his silver-grey Mercedes. Penny was lost, and there was nothing I could do about it. Lina had confided to me on our third date, about the one time the little shit had made a move on her a couple of years ago, and how she had managed to fend him off with the help of one of the waitresses at James' Choice. It was his favorite hunting ground, so the women who worked there were well versed in his luring ways.

It gave me one more reason to admire her spirit and strong survival instincts. I knew I was a very lucky man to be in her life, and suggesting we move in together would be the right thing to do.

## Rockford Summer, 1999

"…it was a hell of a Vienna." The Rat, by Charles Bukowski

it was the summer
of women
an assortment
of women
a plethora
of women
blondes redheads brunettes
coming home from their jobs
the snug fit of pantsuits or skirts
giving me a hint to the many
heated wonders
beneath their thin
layers of fabric

they went inside the three-
story brick bldg across
the street from my apt
where i was holed up
with my books and poems
took off their work clothes
came back outside wearing
tight short shorts
or hip hugging denim
flimsy blouses or t-shirts
looking like erotic tinker
belles in a soft porn movie

i never saw so much leg
sleek legs seen only on

New York runways
fast legs meant to be chased
until they decided to let
me catch them
sturdy legs for dancing in a
smoky bar until 2 a.m.
strong legs to wrestle and
pin me naked panting
to the mattress until
i lived up to my
end of the deal
it was a lonely summer
in a rough town that had
broken better men than me

and sometimes i did
the only thing
that made sense:
curled up on the carpet
bit down on a towel
to stifle my screams
and tears for the lack
of human touch or
the soothing sound
of a woman's voice

but on good days
i had an occasional
9-dollar cigar
a bottle of cheap wine
and a very sweet view
from my 5th flr window

the feeling in my gut
reassuring me

there were better
days to come

# About the Author

Richard Vargas was born in Compton, CA. He earned his B.A. at Cal State University, Long Beach, where he studied under Gerald Locklin and Richard Lee. He edited/published five issues of *The Tequila Review,* 1978-1980, publishing early works by Jimmy Santiago Baca, Alberto Rios, Nila Northsun, Dennis Cooper, Michael C Ford, Ron Koertge, and many more. Books published: *McLife,* (was featured twice in February 2006, on Garrison Keillor's *Writer's Almanac*), *American Jesus,* 2007, *Guernica, revisited,* 2014, (was featured once more on *Writer's Almanac*), *How A Civilization Begins,* 2022, *leaving a tip at the Blue Moon Motel,* 2023, *The Screw City Poems,* July 2025. Vargas received his MFA from the University of New Mexico, 2010, where he workshopped his poetry with Joy Harjo. He was recipient of the 2011 Taos Summer Writers' Conference's Hispanic Writer Award, was on the faculty of the 2012 10th National Latino Writers Conference and facilitated a workshop at the 2015 Taos Summer Writers' Conference. He also edited/published *The Más Tequila Review* from 2009-2015, featuring poets from across the country. His poetry continues to appear in poetry journals and anthologies.

His work history is long and varied. Some of the jobs he's had since the 1970s: fry and grill cook, women's shoes salesman, bank employee, gas station attendant, retail sales/clerk (for house paint, men's clothes, auto service/repair and bookseller), warehouseman, infantry lieutenant, warehouse supervisor, UPS deliveryman, massage therapist, bookstore events coordinator, inbound call center CSR (for several companies). He is now retired but works part-time processing donated clothing at a local Goodwill and is currently hosting a monthly poetry open mic in Madison (Poetry on Tap@Minocqua Brewing Company: "drink beer and don't be racist.") Richard currently resides in Wisconsin, near the lake where Otis Redding's plane crashed.

www.richardvargaspoet.com

# MORE ROADSIDE PRESS TITLES